PRAYERS, PRC
AND PRESCRIPTIONS

By the same author:

Faith, Hope, Love and Laughter – How They Heal (Hale & Iremonger, Sydney, 1999).

Living With Cancer: A Survivor's Guide (Simon & Schuster, Sydney, 2002).

Surviving Mesothelioma and Other Cancers (Cancer Monthly, Inc, North Carolina, 2005).

Prayers, Promises and Prescriptions for Healing

PAUL KRAUS

KINGSWAY PUBLICATIONS
EASTBOURNE

First published 2006

Unless otherwise stated all Bible quotations are from the
New International Version © 1973, 1978, 1984
by the International Bible Society.
NRSV = New Revised Standard Version
NLT = New Living Translation

Thanks to *Wholeness* magazine of the Healing Order
of St Luke, New Zealand, for the poems *Most Richly Blessed*
and *Cancer Is So Limited*.

ISBN 13: 978–1–842912–51–5
ISBN 10: 1 84291 251 8

06 07 80 09 Year/Printing 07 06 05 04 03 02 01

KINGSWAY COMMUNICATIONS LTD
Lottbridge Drove, Eastbourne BN23 6NT, England.
Email: books@kingsway.co.uk

Printed in the USA

Contents

Foreword

The great historian Edward Gibbon in his work *The Decline and Fall of the Roman Empire* said that a major factor in the infant Christian church, that changed it from being a persecuted minority group to being the religion of the Empire under Constantine, was the miraculous in everyday church life.

Prayers, Promises and Prescriptions for Healing makes a substantial contribution to the miraculous being restored in the everyday church life of today. Paul Kraus' presentation very much meets people at their point of felt need. The reader will feel that their personal needs are being understood and addressed in a meaningful way. The reader will see in the pages of this book very clearly that God has made 'precious and great promises' that meet their need – whatever it may be. This book contains simple and clear guidelines to follow that will enable the reader to translate what God provides so that they draw on it in a practical and effective way.

I am pleased to commend Paul Kraus and his fine book to the reading public, and especially to those in need of healing at any level of their being.

Canon Jim Glennon, A.M.
Founder, St. Andrew's Cathedral Healing Ministry, Sydney.

Introduction

All of us are in need of healing. For some the need may be for physical healing and the desperate search to find a cure from a debilitating or life-threatening illness. For others, the need is more for inner healing; the healing of emotions damaged through a negative experience earlier in life. There is a case for the healing of memories. Others are hungering for meaning in their lives and are in need of balance and wholeness. Their daily existence lacks a spiritual dimension.

Many people's lives are brutalized by the sheer complexity of contemporary living with the pressures of its materialist preoccupations. Life seems to have lost its simplicity.

The prayers, meditations, poems and affirmations that follow address our need for healing at all levels: body, mind, spirit and emotions. The bias of this book is strongly and unashamedly biblical, with a strong Christian message running through most of the readings. However, there is a clear recognition that the laws of wellness are universal, not doctrinal. In that sense, this is not a 'religious' book. Jesus' healing ministry transcended doctrine. Rather it focused on forgiveness, faith, hope and love and actually experiencing the power of God in the dark moments of life. Jesus was concerned with healing at all levels, including delivering people from the 'powers of darkness' – demonic influences.

One of the chief criteria for choosing the extracts in this collection is simplicity. Healing is often mistakenly regarded as synonymous with curing. A person can be cured of a serious illness and still have no peace of mind and therefore not have found true healing. Likewise, a person may die from an illness yet still be regarded as having been healed and dying in peace.

This collection on healing aims to help people find healing according to their varied needs. The prayers, affirmations and readings in this book are about life's 'big picture' – life's 'ultimate realities'. They point to the fact that true prayer is tuning into our spiritual essence. Having faith in God and his ultimate goodness generates within us a kind of hope inaccessible by reason. All of us have the potential to experience the power of God within us. This is so at all times but especially in the burdensome moments of life.

Herbert Benson, a professor of medicine at Harvard University, in his book *Timeless Healing* suggests that spirituality heals. He also states that, in spite of his years of scepticism about spiritual things as a medical scientist, he has come to the conclusion that we are 'wired for God' – that we have an innate need to believe in a Being beyond ourselves. Being in touch with our Creator is a vital means of coping with the burden of our mortality.

My hope is that this collection of prayers, biblical verses and commentaries, as well as the biblical affirmations on healing, will not only help people in difficulties on their life journey but will also encourage readers to focus on life's ultimate meaning and purpose.

May the reader experience the touch of God who stands above and beyond the puzzles, tragedies and triumphs of our existence. May those who use this book realize that only God, as revealed in his Son Jesus, can articulate the ultimate truth about who we really are – matter and spirit, body, soul and will. Healing, in both its outward and inner dimensions is all about being made whole in Christ, acknowledging his love and sharing it with others. Essentially, this is what making his kingdom a reality here on earth is all about.

Paul Kraus

My Healing Story

In late June 1997 I was admitted to hospital for a minor routine operation, an umbilical hernia repair. Totally unexpectedly, the surgeon discovered a large amount of fluid in my abdominal cavity. Further investigation revealed what he termed in his report, 'miliary metastatic spread'. In layman's terms, he found that I had extensive and advanced cancerous tumours growing throughout my peritoneum or abdomen. Both the surgeon and the oncologist I was subsequently referred to gave me the bad news that there was nothing medicine had to offer me. They measured my life in months rather than years. I was devastated.

I remember lying in that hospital bed in a state of shock, trying but failing to come to terms with the news that I had just been given. My mind had, as it were, seized. Try as I might, I simply could not pray. Yet, in that short time of anguish I recall with crystal clarity something very beautiful. The words of a hymn I had learned well over forty years earlier came to my mind:

> What a friend we have in Jesus
> All our sins and grief to bear

What a privilege to carry
Everything to God in prayer
O what peace we often forfeit
O what needless pain we bear
All because we do not carry
Everything to God in prayer

As I stared at the hospital ceiling the words of that hymn unwittingly became my prayer. I say 'unwittingly' because I had not sung those words for very many years. Suddenly and so unexpectedly this hymn assumed tremendous comfort and reassurance. Every line was indeed a prescription for coping with this unexpected and dreadful news. I clung dearly to those words. In this darkest grief, the presence of Jesus was very near as each promise of that hymn soaked into my consciousness and brought much comfort. In the coming weeks and months I was to learn that the meaning of healing – at least from a Christian point of view – is Jesus meeting us at our point of need, whatever that need may be.

Since childhood days when I was first taught in Sunday School that Jesus is truly our friend, I had never abandoned my faith in God, although there were times when I had 'wandered from his pathway' and had impetuously gone my own way - living according to my will rather than God's will and robbing myself of peace of mind.

The pathology came back in a couple of weeks and revealed that I was suffering from the asbestos-related cancer called mesothelioma that was incurable. The initial few weeks following the diagnosis was a bewildering and emotionally draining time. We sought further medical opinions, we adopted quite a few self-help techniques and, above all, we prayed for God's power and healing. Within a day of the initial diagnosis our minister came to visit us. Towards the end of his visit he held our hands as we prayed. His prayer was both poignant yet beautiful and I shall always remember it. The theme of his prayer was that nothing could separate us from the love of God in Christ Jesus. He prayed that just as God cares about the sparrow that falls from its nest, so much more does he care about us and that even the hairs on our head are numbered in his sight. He prayed for God's healing power to be very real to us at this time. I felt uplifted and strengthened by the minister's visit. It was like an island of hope in the sea of despair from the awful news we had received earlier that week.

For the first few months my healing journey led me through many dark valleys. The regular tests gave us no joy. Indeed, almost four months after the initial diagnosis, and despite an outpouring of prayer and love from many people, my CT scan showed a marked deterioration. I prayerfully meditated each day, and had adopted a rigorous dietary regime that included large quantities of carrot juice and other juices, a good deal of raw food, as well as an ample intake of fruit and vegetables. I fully and enthusiastically embraced everything I did and wholeheartedly believed that my regime was helping my body to fight this illness. I also felt that God was showing me these things as a means of getting well again. Despite setbacks I was encouraged to persevere in what I was doing. At that time conventional medicine had no answers. I was advised to 'get my house in order'. I read voraciously about every aspect of cancer and, indeed, about the components of health and healing. The love of my family sustained me and I experienced the truth that love has a strong healing effect.

I attended a healing service in Sydney's St Andrew's Cathedral, had the laying-on-of-hands, prayer and anointing. The service was taken by a retired clergyman who was greatly used by God and who had very obviously been given the gift of healing by the Holy Spirit. He preached powerfully on the importance of faith in healing, yet made it clear that faith was not necessarily a pre-condition of healing. Rather, at times it was the faith of others that actually brought about the gift of healing in an individual. Deep down I had a growing conviction that despite the bad news that two professors of oncology had given me, this was not the end of my earthly pilgrimage. At fifty-two years of age God still had work for me. It was a belief that was at times plagued by doubts in the months ahead.

I clung to the precious promises in the word of God and made sure that not a day passed without reading and affirming the truths of various favourite passages. Perhaps the three that resonated most powerfully were (not necessarily in this order):

Romans 15:13: 'May the God of hope fill you with all joy and peace in believing, so that by the power of the Holy Spirit you may abound in hope.' Hope brought joy and peace. Hope is not something illusory to the individual who embraces it with faith and determination, whatever the medical outlook may be. The Holy Spirit, like a dove of peace, was and continues to be, an agent of help and healing, independently of my outward circumstance.

Psalm 27, especially those opening verses of great consolation: 'The Lord is my light and my salvation; whom shall I fear? The Lord is the stronghold of my life: of whom shall I be afraid?' Fear has been one of the worst enemies in my journey with cancer and frequently I turned to this Psalm (as well as Psalm 91) to affirm that I was indeed on a journey of healing and wholeness, wherever that journey was to take me. Healing, I was to discover, was among other things discovering a sense of inner peace, reconnecting with the heart and the soul and walking closely with the Lord. In a sense, it is as simple as that: knowing oneself and knowing and experiencing the power of God in one's life. It is also recognizing that this life is not the final destination. The latter truth is not too difficult to comprehend by anyone diagnosed with a terminal illness.

The third text that I found so strengthening was Mark, 11:22–25: 'Have faith in God. . .' These verses required a deep faith, in believing without any shadow of doubt that God was answering my prayer. It required of me an actual belief that whatever I ask in prayer, I will receive it – if only I believe it will happen. I carefully read all the healing passages in the New Testament and tried to learn about the importance of faith in healing.

The third CT scan was the first to show a halt in the progress of my illness. Meanwhile, my blood tests were not promising. Yet I believed with all my heart that all I was doing to help me get well would take time. I persevered with my regime, especially daily prayer and meditation, daily exercise and an ultra healthy nutritional programme based on a strict 'cancer diet'. I knew full well that diet alone had never cured cancer, yet I also believed that the combination of everything I was doing was playing a vital role. I refused to believe that my condition was incurable. Jesus had healed more than one 'incurable' case.

The fluid in my abdomen was still a problem, but otherwise

I could not say that I felt ill or had any pain. About six months after the initial diagnosis, I intuitively knew that I had 'turned the corner'. I had learnt to live in the present moment, seeing each day as a gift from God. I had learnt to live in a spirit of thankfulness. It seems ironic that it took a life-threatening illness to teach me how to live more mind- fully and more joyfully. It was Albert Einstein who said that there are only two ways to live your life. One is as though nothing is a miracle. The other is as if everything is a mir- acle. This was one of the lessons I learned from living with cancer. For that I thank God.

Some of my fellow sufferers who were diagnosed at roughly the same time as me did not make it. We simply have to admit that we do not know the mind of God in every situation. I do know that each person's situation is unique. Healing is multi-faceted and, as I discovered, relates to body, mind, spirit and emotions. I also know that occa- sionally God heals people spontaneously. From a human perspective healing is a perplexing topic, especially for Christians. We are often tempted to cry out, 'Why wasn't [he/she] healed? They had so many people praying for them, yet it didn't seem to work.' My experience has shown me that Jesus meets us at our point of need, whatever that need may be. It is quite true that sometimes we are mystified by the fact that our prayers don't seem to have been answered – at least, not in the way we expected or hoped for. St Paul reminds us in 1 Corinthians 13:12: 'Now we see but a poor reflection as in a mirror; then we shall see face to face. Now I know in part; then I shall know fully, even as I am fully known.' In 2 Corinthians 4:17–18 he goes on to say: 'For our light and momentary troubles are achieving for us an eternal glory that far outweighs them all. So we fix our eyes not on what is seen, but on what is unseen. For what is seen is temporary, but what is unseen is eternal.' These words and those surrounding them do much to take away the mystery of healing.

I have far outlived my prognosis and have defied the medical odds. My regular CT scans show that my tumours are still there. In the words of the radiologist, 'They don't behave like cancer.' I sometimes wonder whether the tumours are now benign. The doctors are amazed that I am still here. I have not had any conventional medical treatment and I am told that there would not be too many people worldwide who had been diagnosed with advanced mesothelioma who are still living into their eighth year.

I try to live joyously and lovingly and to be of some help to those in need. For each day I live I give thanks and I realize that we all have a 'terminal' prognosis, as Psalm 90, verses 9 and 10 remind us. It is this truth that challenges me to use my time wisely. I give God the glory and thank him that this illness has taught me so much.

Paul Kraus

How to Use This Book

This book aims to inspire its readers with Christian hope and to help all those who are in need of healing, whether of mind, body or emotions.

The quotations, affirmation and prayers also aim to point the reader to those attributes of wellness that help to balance our lives and give greater meaning and joy. It is part of our human condition that we all encounter suffering and pain in one form or another at various points in our lives. What, then, are those things that restore balance and make us whole again?

The apostle Paul gives us the answer when he speaks of the fruits of the Spirit in Galatians 5:22: love, joy, peace, patience, kindness, goodness, gentleness and self-control. The extracts, prayers and promises in this book are largely focused on regaining these fruits of the Spirit that may have been missing in our lives, sometimes through no fault of our own.

Healing, at least from a Christian perspective, is all about Jesus meeting us at our point of need. The word 'healing' is derived from an Old English word meaning 'wholeness'. This is what Jesus' healing ministry was (and is) all about – not merely curing people of their physical infirmities but restoring them to a right relationship with God and with one another.

This book can be used in a number of ways. The reader can use it selectively by referring to the Contents page and choosing those sections that speak to specific needs at any given time, or it can be read through from beginning to end in the normal way.

In other words, it can be used as an inspirational guide to help in times of need or as a devotional aid to focus our thoughts on God's love and the precious promises he has made, as recorded in his holy word, the Bible.

My hope is it can also be used as a handbook, or a more formal devotional book for those who are in any pastoral role, whether as minister, priest, pastoral care worker or carer for those in need of healing or simply for those who really need the sunshine of God's love in their lives.

A number of the promises of healing remind us that God's love is unconditional and that God sometimes heals in ways that we do not expect. Not one character in the Bible died with unanswered prayer, though some died without knowing all the answers (Hebrews 11:39–40). So it is with us. Our task on this earthly journey is to tune in to our spiritual essence through prayer, sometimes vocal, sometimes silent, and to know that God says to us, 'My grace is sufficient for you, for my power is made perfect in weakness' (2 Corinthians 12:9).

1

God's Compassion

The Ministry of Healing

Few words in Christianity are as important as 'compassion'. Jesus' healing ministry was based on compassion. Many times in the Gospel accounts we encounter this great mix of love and mercy which was the hallmark of Jesus' encounter with all those who were suffering in mind, body or spirit.

As followers of Christ, Christians are called upon to show compassion and love demonstrated in acts of kindness and mercy. This is, after all, what the healing ministry is all about. We are called to serve those who are suffering. This is an important manifestation of holiness. In extending compassion we are not only helping those in need, we bring blessing on ourselves.

Service to those who are suffering is at the heart of authentic Christianity:

> Religion that God our Father accepts as pure and faultless is this: to look after orphans and widows in their distress and to keep oneself from being polluted by the world. (James 1:27)

Manifesting God's kindness is an act of holiness, brings us closer to the heart of God and emulates Christ's service:

The Son of Man did not come to be served, but to serve, and to give his life as a ransom for many. (Matthew 20:28)

When we serve those who are in need and who are suffering we are, in reality, serving one part of Christ's body:

If one part suffers, every part suffers with it . . . Now you are the body of Christ, and each of you is part of it . . .(1 Corinthians 12:26–27)

Compassion in action includes praying for those in need, visiting them and showing them acts of mercy. It includes sharing the gospel so that they might find ultimate healing and the kingdom of God through the saving knowledge of Jesus Christ.

Ten Things to Remember When Praying for Healing

1. God wants us to be made whole; God is faithful.
2. God's love is unconditional. We need only to reach out and accept that love.
3. Nothing can ever separate us from the love of God in Christ Jesus.
4. God's love has the power to transform sin, pain and suffering.
5. Being angry with God can in itself be a form of prayer.
6. There is prayer in heartfelt asking, crying and hammering at heaven's door, expecting a response.
7. God seeks us to co-operate with him in our healing journey – whether that journey ends in physical healing or not.
8. We must pray for courage and perseverance to overcome whatever blocks God's healing work in us, especially lack of forgiveness, guilt, resentment and fear.
9. Our final healing will only come when we are born to eternal life through the gate of death.
10. The ultimate goal of healing is to glorify God.

What Do We Mean by Healing?

The word 'healing' means different things to different people. Most of us would regard it as synonymous with curing. The following verse provides a comprehensive array of definitions. This verse quite clearly shows that healing is a state of mind and being, that we need to strive for throughout our lives. Each definition is profound and teaches its own lesson on the ingredients of happiness and wholeness, and living not for oneself but for God and for each other.

Healing Is. . .

HEALING IS filling your mind with God's love and releasing all guilt.

HEALING IS turning towards God and away from disease and depression.

HEALING IS joining your mind and will to God's mind and will.

HEALING IS replacing fear with love, anger with peace, guilt with forgiveness.

HEALING IS seeing yourself as forgiven and taking delight in it.

HEALING IS inner peace which overflows the body.

HEALING IS the same as forgiveness.

HEALING IS thanking God for what he has already given you.

HEALING IS correcting our vision of self, others and God.

HEALING IS reconciliation between mind and spirit.

HEALING IS being humble before God but being powerful in him.

HEALING IS freedom from past guilt and anxiety over the future.

Reproduced with permission of Wholeness *magazine from the 'Healing Order of St. Luke'.*

Circle Me O God

Circle me O God
Keep hope within
Despair without

Circle me O God
Keep peace within
Keep turmoil out

Circle me O God
Keep calm within
Keep storms without

Circle me O God
Keep strength within
Keep weakness out

David Adam,
The Edge of Glory,
Triangle SPCK 1985.

Celtic Prayer

The Lord is here
His Spirit is with us

We need not fear
His Spirit is with us

We are surrounded by love
His Spirit is with us

We are immersed in peace
His Spirit is with us

We abide in hope
His Spirit is with us

We travel in faith
His Spirit is with us

We live in eternity
His Spirit is with us

The Lord is here
His Spirit is with us

David Adam, The Cry of the
Deer, *Triangle/SPCK 1987.*

2

Suffering — A Christian Perspective

God Doesn't Will Suffering

Many people believe in the maxim that eventually everything works out for the best and that worry will not help. As true as this might be, the reality is that things don't always 'work out for the best' in our lifetime. Ask the parents of a young child who succumbs to leukaemia or a close relative of an accident victim. There are certainly times when suffering has an inexplicable mysterious dimension. Ultimately, the fact remains that God does not will suffering or tragedy. It is the inevitable result of living in a world subject to sin, disease and death. Our idea of 'things working out for the best' may not be the same as God's. Not infrequently, God's ultimate purposes are, at least in the short term, hidden from our eyes. This is not synonymous with blind faith but has to do with trusting in the loving, just and faithful character of our sovereign God.

So then, what is the Christian response to suffering? In brief, it is simply that when all human resources fail there is a loving wisdom and an Almighty power active within us who is capable of raising our life to a new level. St Paul summed up this idea perfectly when he wrote:

So we do not lose heart. Even though our outer nature is wasting away, our inner nature is being renewed day by day. For this slight momentary affliction is preparing us for an eternal weight of glory beyond all measure, because we look not at what can be seen but at what cannot be seen; for what can be seen is temporary, but what cannot be seen is eternal. (2 Corinthians 4:16–18 NRSV)

As Christians we believe that Jesus, our Messiah and Saviour, overcame suffering, and death itself, so we have an assurance that Jesus is with us in whatever situation we find ourselves. In other words, we are not the plaything of fate or circumstance. That is the only reasonable answer the Christian can offer to the mystery of suffering.

We can take heart in the knowledge that at times of desolation and suffering only God knows and understands our pain. It is precisely at those times that God's power is working in us to sustain and uphold us: 'I am with you always, to the very end of the age' (Matthew 28:20).

When we are at the end of our tether, when life seems to be altogether overwhelming, we need to realize that 'God's power is working in us'. This is the power the disciples experienced in their desolation after Jesus their Lord had been crucified.

No, in all these things we are more than conquerors through him who loved us. For I am convinced that neither death nor life, neither angels nor demons, neither the present nor the future, nor any powers, neither height nor depth, nor anything else in all creation, will be able to separate us from the love of God that is in Christ Jesus our Lord. (Romans 8:37–39)

Biblical Prescriptions

The Lord is my light and my salvation – whom shall I fear?
The Lord is the stronghold of my life – of whom shall I be afraid?
My heart says of you, 'Seek his face!'
Your face, Lord, I will seek.
Do not hide your face from me, do not turn your servant away in anger; you have been my helper.
Do not reject me or forsake me, O God my Saviour.
Wait for the Lord; be strong and take heart and wait for the Lord. (Psalm 27:1, 8–9, 14)

Even though I walk through the valley of the shadow of death, I will fear no evil, for you are with me; your rod and your staff, they comfort me. (Psalm 23:4)

For he will command his angels concerning you to guard you in all your ways; they will lift you up in their hands, so that you will not strike your foot against a stone. (Psalm 91:11–12)

My grace is sufficient for you, for my power is made perfect in weakness. (2 Corinthians 12:9)

Suffering – Traversing the River

And I saw the river
Over which every soul must pass
To reach the kingdom of heaven
And the name of that river was suffering –
And I saw the boat
Which carries souls across the river
And the name of that boat was
Love

St John of the Cross, Christian mystic.

How to Cope in a Time of Suffering

Christians, like everyone else, face times of suffering in their life. Such occasions can be overwhelming, almost too much to bear. Yet times of trial can also be key turning points in a Christian's walk with God. We have the choice of either turning to the Lord in complete trust and surrender, or we can sink into a quagmire of despair. Our faith can either be a source of strength or it can fail the test. In the latter situation we can blame ourselves or we can be angry with God. Fear and confusion can play havoc with our faith. Fear is the enemy of faith. In times of fear we can forget that *nothing* can separate us from God.

In times of trial we would do well to remember that suffering is a path to holiness. In other words, suffering can be a path to becoming more Christ-like. It is through perseverance – an undying faith in our Lord's promise that he will never leave us – that we will find blessing in the midst of our suffering. Paul reassures us that the Spirit helps us in our weakness: '. . . for we do not know how to pray as we ought, but the Spirit himself intercedes for us with sighs too deep for words' (Romans 8:26 RSV). God is in the midst of our suffering and we therefore have no need to fear.

When we surrender our suffering to the Lord Jesus Christ we will less easily fall into depression and despair. It is only then that we can ultimately know that 'all things work together for good to those who love him and are called according to his purposes'. We may not know what that purpose might be for now, but we have God's assurance that one day we will see him as he is.

The reasons we are confronted by suffering are many and varied. Sometimes it might be because of sin, either our own or others. It might be because Satan is attacking us. Then again, the reason might not be apparent in the short term. In life's 'big picture' we are forced to concede that suffering is within the realm of God's providence. What we need to realize above all else is that God's grace is sufficient to meet all our needs. He sustains us in our weakness and through the experience of suffering we are made more holy and more Christ-like.

Prayers for those Experiencing Suffering and Pain

Loving God,
I bring before you all those who are suffering at this time,
All those who feel overwhelmed by their situation,
    especially [Name].
Help them to let go into your life-giving power.
Help them not to lose heart.
Enable them to see Jesus, who has overcome the world.
May your Holy Spirit, like a dove,
Come upon them now to strengthen and comfort them
    wherever they may be.
Help them to see that even death itself is but a new
    beginning.
These things I pray through the precious name of Jesus,
Who has overcome the world,
Amen

May the pain of God be the gift of life to you.
May the suffering of Jesus be the threshold of joy to you.
May the travail of the Spirit be a prelude to a birthing for
    you.

May the inexpressible joy of meeting him face to face bring you his peace.

Amen

Paul Kraus

Suffering – God's Irony

Our life is a short time in expectation, a time in which sadness and joy kiss each other at every moment. There is a quality of sadness that pervades all the moments in our life. It seems that there is no such thing as a clear-cut pure joy, but that even in the most happy moments of our existence we sense a tinge of sadness. In every satisfaction there is an awareness of limitations. In every success, there is the fear of jealousy. Behind every smile, there is a tear. In every embrace, there is loneliness. In every friendship, distance. And in all forms of light, there is knowledge of surrounding darkness . . .

But this intimate experience in which every bit of life is touched by a bit of death can point us beyond the limits of our existence. It can do so by making us look forward in expectation to the day when our hearts will be filled with perfect joy, a joy that no one can take away from us.

Henri Nouwen, Making All Things New: An Invitation to the Spiritual Life. *Harper & Row, 1981, p.51.*

Used with permission.

Cancer Is So Limited . . .

It cannot cripple love,
It cannot shatter hope,
It cannot corrode faith,
It cannot remove peace,
It cannot destroy confidence,
It cannot kill friendship,
It cannot shut out memories,
It cannot silence courage,
It cannot invade the soul,
It cannot reduce eternal life,
It cannot quench the Spirit,
It cannot lessen the power of the resurrection . . .
Our greatest enemy is not the disease,
But despair.
Keep trusting God's love so your spirit will remain strong.

Harold Larsen, cancer patient.
Reproduced with permission of Wholeness *magazine.*

3

Faith and Trust

The Paradox of Faith

In some ways faith is a paradox. It is essentially a simple thing – a matter of complete trust; a strongly held belief, irrespective of whether or not logical proof exists. The very simplicity of having a childlike faith is its greatest stumbling block. We sometimes confuse faith with wishful thinking, which means we are incapable of 'letting go and letting God'. When we undergo trials in life, the strength of our faith is tested.

The great person of faith as far as suffering is concerned was Job in the Bible. He stands as an archetype of faith, although, of course, in an altogether different way from Moses or Abraham. Anyone who is familiar with the book of Job will readily agree. Faith, like suffering, can never be fully understood in this life. A strong faith in God and in his Son Jesus Christ is never a guarantee that physical healing will take place, although it is frequently a precondition for healing. The truth of this is clearly shown in the record of Jesus' healing ministry, especially in Luke's Gospel.

What we *can* know with absolute certainty is the record of God's faithfulness with those who have a living relationship with him. It is good to remember that there was not one person in the entire Bible who ended their life with unanswered prayer though their faith was tested. People like Abraham, Moses, Jacob, Isaac, Elijah, Amos, Hosea and a great many others were people of great faith who all experienced a close walk with God. Nowhere in the Bible is God's faithfulness better expressed than in the Psalms of David, where he expresses in such an intimate way a range of emotions in his response to God's dealings with him.

The focus of our faith should always be on God and his wisdom to help and heal us in the way that only he knows will be for our ultimate good. Perhaps the most comprehensive summary of faith is found in Hebrews 11: 'Now faith is the assurance of things hoped for, the conviction of things not seen . . .' (RSV). The writer goes on to chronicle a long list of examples of the faith of the patriarchs, such as Abraham and Moses. At the end of these examples of people of faith, the writer states: 'And all these, though well attested by their faith, did not receive what was promised, since God had foreseen something better for us' (Hebrews 11:39 RSV).

God is faithful to his promises to hear and answer our prayers, although not necessarily in the way we expect. We need to learn to trust God in the assurance that he loves us unconditionally and that he will 'never leave us nor forsake us'. Ultimately, our faith must be in God and in his wisdom and power, and not in our own faith. Our faith and love fluctuates with circumstance; God's love never changes: 'I am with you always, to the very end of the age' (Matthew 28:20).

Psalm 23 – Living in a Deep Faith with the Living God

The Lord is my shepherd, I shall not be in want.
He makes me lie down in green pastures,
he leads me beside quiet waters,
he restores my soul.
He guides me in paths of righteousness for his name's
    sake.
Even though I walk through the valley of the shadow of
    death,
I will fear no evil, for you are with me;
your rod and your staff, they comfort me.
You prepare a table before me in the presence of my
    enemies.
You anoint my head with oil; my cup overflows.
Surely goodness and love will follow me
all the days of my life,
and I will dwell in the house of the Lord
for ever.

Meditation on Psalm 23

Do you only call upon God's help in times of trouble or is God the shepherd of your life in every situation?

Do you believe that God's love for you is unconditional?

Are you ready to 'let go and let God' and therefore find healing in those areas of your life where you know that healing needs to take place?

Have you let go of past resentments and bitterness? Do you need to forgive others or yourself for past wrongs?

Do you live in the present and look to God each day for guidance?

A Prayer for Faith Based on Psalm 23

Lord, there are times when I really wonder what my faith is all about. There are times when I wonder why you hide your purposes from me, when darkness and gloom crowd in on my life. Lord, help me in my unbelief. Lord, may I always walk by faith and not by sight, knowing that you will never leave me or forsake me. I will fear no evil for you are with me. May I live the reality of these words in my daily walk. Grant me a spirit of thankfulness rather than a spirit of despair. May I know that love always triumphs over evil, just as Jesus triumphed over the cross. I surrender to you my cares and burdens and leave them all at the foot of the cross. May your holy angels watch over me and those whom I love. In Jesus' name I pray.
     Amen.

Psalm 27 – A Prayer of Trust and Affirmation

The Lord is my light and my salvation – whom shall I fear?
The Lord is the stronghold of my life – of whom shall I be
    afraid? . . .
Though an army besiege me, my heart will not fear . . .
One thing I ask of the Lord, this is what I seek:
that I may dwell in the house of the Lord all the days of
    my life . . .
For in the day of trouble he will keep me safe in his
    dwelling;
he will hide me in the shelter of his tabernacle and set me
    high upon a rock. . .
Hear my voice when I call, O Lord;
be merciful to me and answer me . . .
Do not hide your face from me . . .
you have been my helper . . . I am still confident of this:
I will see the goodness of the Lord in the land of the
    living.
Wait for the Lord; be strong and take heart and wait for
    the Lord.

Meditation on Psalm 27

Faith is a channel for healing to take place. Faith, love and fear cannot co-exist. Do you believe the Lord is your light and salvation and not just an emotional or spiritual 'band-aid'? Is the Lord a living presence in your daily walk?

A Healing Meditation

In our weakest times God's strength is ours to trust;
In our saddest times his compassion is ours to heal;
In all times his love is ours to share.

Why Faith Heals

Why, indeed, does faith heal? Or perhaps we might ask how faith heals? There is, at one level at least, no simple answer to a mysterious and complex question.

A Christian response to why faith heals will take the line that God, through Jesus, loved us so much that he made atonement for our sin on the cross and that all those who believe on the Lord Jesus Christ will find forgiveness and healing. The wonderful thing about God's forgiveness in Christ is that as soon as we sincerely repent of our sins and seek God's forgiven we can know for certain that our sins are forgiven and that we are released from the power they held over us. Healing, on the other hand, takes time and is a gradual process of being made whole once again.

In the Gospels Jesus performed a number of healings on people whose faith and trust in him was strong. For example, Jesus healed the woman who had been suffering from a haemorrhage for twelve years. In faith she touched the edge of Jesus' cloak expecting a miracle. In compassion Jesus turned to her and said, 'Take heart, daughter, your faith has healed you' (Matthew 9:22). Instantly the woman was healed of her infirmity.

Likewise, in the book of the Acts of the Apostles we read of the poor crippled beggar whom Peter healed by faith in the power of the risen Jesus: 'By faith in the name of Jesus, this man whom you see and know was made strong. It is Jesus' name and the faith that comes through him that has given this complete healing to him, as you can all see' (Acts 3:16).

We also know from Scripture that faith in the Son of God is a means by which we can overcome the vicissitudes of life: 'For everyone born of God overcomes the world. This is the victory that has overcome the world, even our faith' (1 John 5:4).

Faith and hope go hand in hand. Christians have ample grounds for hope: 'For God so loved the world that he gave his one and only Son, that whoever believes in him shall not perish but have eternal life' (John 3:16). This is not some 'pie in the sky' hope. Rather, it is a hope based on historical reality on the life and death of Jesus. Our present worries and sufferings pale in comparison to the wonder of God's ultimate promises.

Believe With Your Heart

'Have faith in God,' Jesus answered. 'I tell you the truth, if anyone says to this mountain, "Go throw yourself into the sea," and does not doubt in his heart but believes that what he says will happen, it will be done for him. Therefore I tell you, whatever you ask in prayer, believe that you will receive it, and it will be yours. And when you stand praying, if you hold anything against anyone, forgive him, so that your Father in heaven may forgive you your sins.' (Mark 11, 22–25)

A Prayer to Act on this Promise

Loving God,

Help me to take these words of Jesus to heart. You see, the problem is that I find it so hard to believe. For so long I have treated you as a band-aid to patch things up in times of trouble. Now I feel a sense of guilt. I feel like a hypocrite asking you for help. I recognize my weakness, Lord. Forgive me for the times I have ignored you and ignored my brothers and sisters in need. Accept me as I am in all my helplessness.

Lord, I so much want to believe your love for me. Help me now to 'let go and let God' – to let go of my fear, my guilt and to believe in your loving power to heal. Free me from myself and let me cast myself on your goodness. All my crises will pass, but your steadfast power and love remain eternal. Grant me the gift of faith and the power of hope that goes with it.

I ask this in the name of Jesus, my brother, my Saviour, friend and redeemer.

Amen.

Trusting in God's Goodness and Wisdom

We cannot expect to know healing in our lives, or in the lives of those for whom we are praying, unless we learn to 'let go and let God'; unless we are freed from the tyranny of our own doubts and fears and surrender to the goodness of God, knowing that he loves us and wants our ultimate good. At the same time we need to be aware that life at times is mysterious and its problems and puzzles do not lend themselves to easy, glib explanations . . . 'for my ways are not your ways, says the Lord'. The kingdom of this world is far removed from the kingdom of God.

Paul summarized the puzzles of this world when he wrote: 'Now we see but a poor reflection as in a mirror; then we shall see face to face. Now I know in part; then I shall know fully, even as I am fully known' (1 Corinthians 13:12).

What we can know with absolute certainty is that God understands us better than we know ourselves; that he loves us and that his power will accomplish our needs. The difficulty is simply in taking a leap of faith and believing that, although we cannot always understand the purposes of God, he will never leave us or forsake us and that underneath we will always be held in his everlasting arms.

We need to learn the art of letting go; in leaving the results of our prayers in his keeping. We need to have the courage to set out on a journey of faith, believing that God is always faithful to his promises and that 'love never fails'. Faith is not about being certain that our prayers are going to be answered in the way we expect. While we cannot know where our journey will take us, we can know with absolute certainty that he loves us.

4

Knowing the Peace of God

Attaining Peace of Mind

'The mind controlled by the Spirit is life and peace' (Romans 8:6). Our inner attitudes affect every part of our life, including our physical health. Our inner 'climate' reflects the balance, or imbalance, in our life. We are spirit, soul and body. If one part of our system is affected then other parts will also suffer. The attitudes we have do not stay in our minds as mere attitudes, they have physical manifestations. God made us this way. He gave us the Ten Commandments not merely as moral rules to live by but as signposts for healthy living. A surgeon once said, 'I've discovered that the kingdom of God is at the end of my scalpel; it's in the tissues. The right thing morally is the right thing physically.'

The laws of morality and the laws of health are written by the same God for the same purpose – healthy and happy living. The Bible has much to say about how to attain peace. Jesus said to his disciples, 'Peace I leave with you; my peace I give you; I do not give to you as the world gives. Do not let your hearts be troubled and do not be afraid' (John 14:27). Paul calls peace one of the fruits of the Spirit (Galatians 5:22). Peace is the product of walking closely with

God. Isaiah said, 'You will keep in perfect peace all who trust in you, whose thoughts are fixed on you!' (Isaiah 26:3 NLT).

Sometimes, particularly in the Old Testament, the Bible associates peace with our welfare, an external thing. At other times, especially in the New Testament, peace has more to do with our inward state. Whatever the context of the Bible's teaching about peace, it is always dependent on being attuned to the presence of the living God in our lives and in doing his will.

Peace and joy go hand in hand. Joy can come from helping and being helped; it can come from redefining – or discovering – life's goal. It can also come from a loving relationship, or from the joy of giving and receiving. Above all, joy comes from being at peace with God and at peace with ourselves. St Augustine once wrote, 'Our hearts are restless until they find their rest in you.' To have a vital, living relationship with Jesus and to feel the power of his Spirit in our lives is the surest way of finding peace, irrespective of whatever adversity may befall us.

Finding Peace in Jesus

Peace, perfect peace, in this dark world of sin?
The Blood of Jesus whispers peace within.
Peace, perfect peace, by thronging duties pressed?
To do the will of Jesus, this is rest.
Peace, perfect peace, with sorrows surging round?
On Jesus' bosom nought but calm is found.
Peace, perfect peace, with loved ones far away?
In Jesus' keeping we are safe, and so are they.
Peace, perfect peace, our futures all unknown?
Jesus we know, and He is on the throne.
Peace, perfect peace, death shadowing us and ours?
Jesus has vanquished death and all its powers.
It is enough: earth's struggles soon shall cease,
And Jesus calls us to heaven's perfect peace.

From The Book of Common Praise,
with Australian Supplement.
Reproduced with permission of Oxford University Press.

The Peace of God

Peace! The very word has a soothing ring to it. Peace of mind is an essential ingredient of healing, of body, mind, spirit and emotions. A well-known American doctor was quoted as saying that what's in your mind is often quite literally or anatomically in your body. That's why there is frequently a close correlation between your mental and physical health. Blockages to healing include resentment, hate, guilt, anger or any other strife. These negative emotions are injurious to our health and will certainly disturb our peace of mind. 'A cheerful heart is good medicine, but a crushed spirit dries up the bones' (Proverbs 17:22).

The prophet Isaiah wrote, 'You will keep in perfect peace all who trust in you.' The phrase 'perfect peace' rules out anxiety and replaces it with a rock-solid trust in God's infinite wisdom, love and power. Paul reminds us that God is 'able to do immeasurably more than all we ask or imagine, according to his power that is at work within us' (Ephesians 3:20). It is only when we have faith in God's goodness that we can apprehend his power to overrule any unfavourable outward circumstance. Only by resting in the love of God can we know deep peace. Often we simply cannot rest in the love of God because we are too tense and therefore lack inner peace. So, how can we start to experience God's presence within? Two practical suggestions will help you get started.

The first way to acquire this inner stillness is to sit in a peaceful environment and to enter a state of silence. Gently close your eyes, take a few deep audible breaths, sigh aloud and then actually say aloud, 'I am now in the presence of God. I leave aside all care and worry. I am still and peaceful. God is my strength and shield.'

Sit for a few minutes in this stillness. If your mind jumps from thought to thought (as it probably will), simply focus attention on your breath. Visualize your breath entering and leaving your body. This exercise – sitting in stillness – in surrender to God, is a simple form of contemplative prayer, putting yourself in God's presence. In this state of being you will never find yourself assailed by outward conflict.

'I have told you these things, so that in me you may have peace. In this world you will have trouble. But take heart! I have overcome the world.' (John 16:33)

The peace of God, which transcends all understanding, will guard your hearts and your minds in Christ Jesus. (Philippians 4:7)

A Meditation on Peace

Deep peace of the running wave to you.
Deep peace of the flowing air to you.
Deep peace of the quiet earth to you.
Deep peace of the shining stars to you.
Deep peace of the Son of Peace to you.

A Celtic blessing

Lord Jesus Christ, you said to your apostles:
'I leave you peace, my peace I give to you.'
Look not on our sins, but on the faith of your Church,
And grant us the peace and unity of your kingdom
Where you live for ever and ever.
Amen

A prayer before Communion

'The soul is immediately at one with God, when it is truly at
peace with itself.'

Julian of Norwich

A Prescription for Anxiety

Anxiety, worry and stress have both positive and negative sides to them. 'Positive' stress can spur us to action when action is called for. Worry and stress brought on by deep-seated fear is, on the contrary, emotionally draining and unhealthy. Sometimes drugs alleviate stress and worry. The Bible has a clear prescription for stress and worry. In Matthew's Gospel, 6:25–34, Jesus sets out five reasons why we should not worry:

(1) Worry clearly shows that our faith is weak

Faith and worry are incompatible. The more we have faith and trust in God the less we will be worrying; the more we worry the less we trust in God. Jesus' assurance that we need not worry is unambiguous when he said: 'Look at the birds of the air; they do not sow or reap or store away in barns, and yet your heavenly Father feeds them. Are you not much more valuable than they?'

(2) Worrying adversely affects our relationship with God

After all, we have been created to have a living relationship with a God who cares for us so much that he gave his Son to die for us in order that our relationship to our heavenly Father might be restored. Therefore, life is, indeed, all about that relationship. Worry is one of the negative emotions that gets in the way of that relationship.

(3) Worrying is an unnecessary burden

Jesus makes this point very clearly in the passage of Matthew's Gospel quoted above when he said: 'Therefore do not worry about tomorrow, for tomorrow will worry about itself. Each day has enough trouble of its own' (Matthew 6:34).

(4) Worrying is contrary to trusting God's goodness

We should not be worried over the things of this world: 'Seek first his kingdom and his righteousness, and all these things will be given to you as well.' Worry and anxiety negate our dependence on God.

(5) It's a waste of time to worry

Much of what consumes us in worry never happens. How often we worry about a certain eventuality that looms like the sword of Damocles over our head, only to realize in due course that our worry was unnecessary.

The word of God exhorts us on a number of occasions to leave our worry in God's care:

> Humble yourselves, therefore, under God's mighty hand, that he may lift you up in due time. Cast all your anxiety on him because he cares for you. (1 Peter 5:7)

Cast your cares on the Lord and he will sustain you; he will never let the righteous fall. (Psalm 55:22)

Do not be anxious about anything, but in everything, by prayer and petition, with thanksgiving, present your requests to God. (Philippians 4:6)

Always try to live in the present moment; not in the past or the future. It has been said 'Yesterday is history, tomorrow is a mystery, but today is a gift – that's why it's called "the present".'

> All your anxiety, all your care,
> Bring to the mercy seat, leave it there;
> Never a burden he cannot bear,
> Never a friend like Jesus.

A Prayer for Serenity and Courage

Dear Lord,
Help me to live this day
Quietly, easily;
To lean upon your strength
Trustfully, restfully;
To wait for the unfolding of your will
Patiently, serenely;
To meet others
Peacefully, joyously;
To face tomorrow
Confidently, courageously.
These things I pray through
Jesus' Name
Amen

Let Nothing Disturb You

Let nothing disturb you
Let nothing frighten you
All things pass away
God alone is changeless.
Patient endurance attains all things.
The one whom God possesses
Lacks nothing
For God alone suffices.

St Teresa of Avila

5

Prayer — Our Spiritual Essence

What Is Prayer?

Countless volumes have been written on the subject down through the ages. Prayer has been defined in a great many ways. These include speaking to God and listening to him. Prayer is focusing on an intention, a desire or a particular situation. In prayer we seek to draw close to God. Words are not an essential ingredient of prayer. Contemplating a beautiful sunset can be a form of prayer. Silence can be a form of prayer. A loving touch can be a prayer.

Prayer has the capacity to change us and the way in which we view the world. Indeed, true prayer ought to change the person who is praying. Faith is a component of prayer. As the writer of the book of Hebrews says: 'Faith is the substance of things hoped for, the evidence of things not seen' (Hebrews11:1 KJV).

For prayer to be effective we need to have a faith that *believes* prayer is being answered, even if not in the way we expect, for God is greater than our hearts and he knows everything (1 John 3:20). It is only when we believe that God is in every situation that we can say with St Paul, 'We know that in all things God works for the good of those who love him, who have been called according to his purpose'

(Romans 8:28). Even in the most tragic situations God has a higher purpose that is clouded from our sight. We need to learn to place our burdens, our joys and all our concerns at the foot of the cross, rather than be consumed by them. It is not surprising that sometimes we are inattentive to God's answer to our prayer and fail to recognize it.

If we pray in a spirit of acceptance and surrender we know that God will always hear our prayer. He has promised that this is the case in his word, the Bible:

> Ask and it will be given to you; seek and you will find; knock and the door will be opened to you. For everyone who asks receives: he who seeks finds; and to him who knocks, the door will be opened. (Matthew 7:7)

There are many other promises and assurances in Scripture that God is 'our very present help in trouble' as well as being the shepherd of our souls. A childlike faith in the goodness, strength and nearness of God is something that can spread an abiding peace and calm into every situation we face. If we only use God like a spiritual 'band-aid' we need not be surprised if our prayers don't seem to 'work'. Nor is God someone with whom we bargain. Yet, even when we have a close walk with our loving heavenly Father we need to realize that God's ways are not our ways, but he answers prayers for our ultimate good. That might be perplexing in the short term. We would do well to live St Paul's words in every situation of our lives: 'Do not be anxious about anything, but in everything, by prayer and petition, with thanksgiving, present your requests to God' (Philippians 4:6).

Faith in the Power of Prayer

Prayer is a powerful means by which we can find peace and healing whatever our circumstances. God's providential care is all-sustaining. It is only when we pray with absolute unwavering trust, believing that God is with us in every situation of life, that we can experience the peace which Paul describes as 'surpassing all understanding'.

The apostle James expressed this so clearly when he said: 'And the prayer offered in faith will make the sick person well; the Lord will raise him up. If he has sinned, he will be forgiven' (James 5:15).

The prophet Isaiah encourages us to 'Seek the Lord while he may be found, call upon him while he is near . . .' (55:6). Isaiah went on to plead with his hearers to return to the Lord and seek his forgiveness. Forgiveness and being in a right relationship with the Lord is an essential ingredient of healing. We cannot enjoy peace of mind when we experience guilt.

To pray is to tune into our spiritual essence – the very core of our being. The Psalms eloquently testify to the ways in which prayer is life-sustaining. Every emotion – joy, anger, despair and gratitude, as well as the wonder of life itself – is contained within its pages. The Psalms are a clear testament to answered prayer.

The gift of prayer is peace and healing, in the fullest sense of that term. Prayer is such a powerful force for good. Prayer is opening the door of your life to God. Prayer is not an exercise in wishful thinking. Rather it is an act of surrendering to God and drawing closer to him. Prayer changes things, even when we may not (especially in the short term) know how.

Releasing Healing in Prayer

Emotional problems such as bitterness, resentment and guilt are often associated with poor mental and physical health. Therefore addressing emotional problems is an important priority for healing to take place. We need to pray for the Lord's forgiveness, cleansing and healing power to enter those aspects of our lives (such as unresolved guilt and painful memories) which block our healing. Inner healing and deliverance from evil influences can be a precondition of healing. Sometimes to obtain inner healing you need to speak to someone you can trust and who is professionally competent to help you. Seek out a Christian counsellor, pastor or priest with whom you would feel comfortable; this is very important in your healing journey.

A Prayer for Healing

God our Father, you are the source of all life and health, all strength and peace. Teach me your ways and fill me with your love. Take from me and those for whom I pray all that hinders your healing power: all sins, anxieties, fear, resentment, burdens and hardness of heart. May I lose myself in the ocean of your love.

Help me to enter into stillness and peace with you and to experience your healing power. This I pray through my friend, my Saviour, my Redeemer, Jesus my Lord.

Amen.

A Further Prayer for Healing

Lord, be my healing. As I pray for myself and for [name] give me complete confidence in your power to heal in the way you know it needs to take place. Help us to work in harmony with you, not against you. Remove from me and from [name] all that obstructs your loving power to heal. In place of anger, hurt, bitterness, failure to forgive, fill me [or name] with Love, Joy, Peace, Kindness, Goodness, Faithfulness, Gentleness and Self-control. Let these grow in me, and in [name], and be the signs of healing through Jesus Christ our Lord.

Amen.

From the Anglican Parish of Fremantle,
Healing Ministry Bookmark, Western Australia.

A Paraphrase of the Perfect Healing Prayer

Our gracious and loving Father in heaven, your name is
holy and to be honoured and praised at all times.
Help me to hasten the coming of your kingdom by doing
your will.
In your mercy give me my daily bread, both physical and
spiritual.

May I experience your forgiveness
   for the times I fail you and fail my brothers and sisters.
Give me strength of character to forgive those who have
   in any way harmed me.
Save me from the time of trial and deliver me from evil.
For the kingdom, the power and the glory are yours, both
   now and forevermore.
Amen.

A Simple Prayer for Healing

> Lord, I believe in you.
> Lord, I hope in you.
>
> Lord, I love you.
> Lord, hear me.
>
> Lord, make me whole.
> Lord, increase my faith.
>
> Lord Jesus Christ,
> Son of the living God,
> Have mercy on me.

Unanswered Prayer

Doubt and fear negate the effects of prayer. In the Gospel of Mark Jesus spoke of faith so strong that it can move mountains. The apostle James exhorted his readers to 'believe and not doubt, because he who doubts is like a wave of the sea, blown and tossed by the wind' (James 1:6).

It can be exceedingly trying if our heartfelt prayers are apparently not being answered. Walking by faith and not by sight does not mean that we deny that circumstances are the way they are. Rather it means that we believe, act, think and talk as though our prayers have been answered. The fact remains that prayer changes things, even when we cannot immediately see how. By praying that God will come into your life, you have absolute certainty that he will empower you to meet any challenge that life might bring. God is with you in your pain and suffering. He will shelter you in the shadow of his wing, as the Psalmist declared (Psalms 36, 57, 63, 91).

Jesus commanded us: 'Ask and it shall be given to you; seek and you will find; knock and the door will be opened to you. For everyone who asks receives; he who seeks finds; and to him who knocks, the door will be opened' (Matthew

7:7). If we heed this command we need not worry about the ultimate outcome of our prayers. We need only to ask our heavenly Father for healing, in whatever form it needs to take place.

'Therefore I tell you, whatever you ask in prayer, believe that you have received it, and it will be yours.' (Mark 11:24)

So we fix our eyes not on what is seen, but on what is unseen. For what is seen is temporary, but what is unseen is eternal. (2 Corinthians 4:18)

We live by faith, not by sight. (2 Corinthians 5:7)

Faith is being sure of what we hope for and certain of what we do not see. (Hebrews 11:1)

Most Richly Blessed

I asked for strength that I might achieve;
I was made weak that I might learn humbly to obey.
I asked for health that I might do greater things;
I was given infirmity that I might do better things.
I asked for riches that I might be happy;
I was given poverty that I might be wise.
I asked for power that I might have the praise of men;
I was given weakness that I might feel the need of God.
I asked for all things that I might enjoy life;
I was given life that I might enjoy all things.
I got nothing that I had asked for, but everything I had
　　hoped for.
Almost despite myself, my unspoken prayers were
　　answered;
I am among all men most richly blessed.

Prayer composed by an unknown Confederate
soldier between 1861 and 1865.
Reproduced by permission of Wholeness *magazine.*

6

The Importance of
Forgiveness in Healing

Forgiveness – Liberating the Soul

As with the choice regarding the attitudes we hold, so too we have a choice when it comes to forgiveness. We can either go on living with feelings of resentment and hurt or we can choose to forgive the person who has hurt us. Forgiveness can be a particularly difficult thing to do and, as with the case of seeking inner healing, we may require professional help – but it is an important part of the healing process at any level: body, mind or emotion. What then, do we understand forgiveness to mean?

It is not burying or denying our hurt. Neither is it forgetting the wrongs of the past and merely saying that everything is now alright, although forgetting forms a part of forgiving. Forgiveness is a process – that of healing damaged emotions by growing beyond them. It is not something we do from coercion or compulsion but is a liberating process that we want to go through.

Learning to Forgive

Learning to forgive is not easy but there are a number of steps that might help you. The first is to recognize your hurt and the bondage in which this hurt is holding you. At times this hurt might be buried in your subconscious. Therefore, in order to adequately deal with it, you may need to seek professional guidance from a Christian counsellor, particularly if the matter is serious and goes back many years, even decades.

The second step is to accept the fact that you are hurting and confront this hurt by acknowledging the anger and pain and confronting it. Then resolve, with God's help, to let go of the past, let go of negative feelings, both in your mind and in your heart. Try to have a sense of compassion towards the person who hurt you. Try to understand why that person behaved in the way they did. Were they themselves victims of circumstance?

The third step is to commit the issue to the Lord. Pray the Lord's Prayer slowly and deliberately, recalling the way Jesus forgave those who 'trespassed against him'. Regularly ask Jesus' help to release you from your burden of anger, guilt and shame about having been hurt or having hurt another. Only by making a genuine effort to change your heart can you move forward. The only way to release negative emotions is to see those who have hurt us as God himself sees them – as people who are loved despite their sinful ways.

If the person is not sorry for what they did, and is even continuing to hurt others, you may find it hard to forgive because you feel it is somehow unfair and they should not be allowed to 'get away with it'. However, do not forget that God is just and we will all stand before him to give an account of ourselves on judgement day. God still asks that you forgive them. 'It is *mine* to avenge; *I* will repay' says the

Lord (Deuteronomy 32:35). 'Do not judge, and you will not be judged. Do not condemn, and you will not be condemned. Forgive, and you will be forgiven' (Luke 6:37). It can't be clearer than that.

Prayers for Forgiveness

Lord Jesus, you taught us that we can only be forgiven, as we ourselves learn to forgive. Keep us mindful of our own shortcomings and sinfulness. As we remember the hurts that we have suffered and never merited, may we also be mindful of the kindnesses we have received and never earned. Remind us always of your great love. May we for ever dwell in that perfect love and so come to know that peace which passes all understanding. Through Jesus Christ our Lord.
Amen.

God of all mercy, teach us to be merciful,
Even indeed as you are merciful.
God of all forgiveness, help us to forgive others,
As you have forgiven us.
Make us aware that in the measure we mete out to others
It shall be measured against us.
Release us from the bondage of lingering resentment
And bitterness, which can only do us harm.
May the fire of your love purge away all hurt
And bring healing where it is needed.
May your Holy Spirit, like a dove,

Make his dwelling place in our hearts.

If we have been hurt,
Grant us your peace and your strength
To overcome that injury;
If we have hurt another,
Grant us your forgiveness and
Set us free from guilt and shame
Until at last we can experience your peace –
A peace that passes all understanding.

This we ask in the precious name of the one
Who sets us free,
Even your Son,
Our Lord and Saviour Jesus Christ.
Amen.

Decide to Forgive

In order to allow healing to take place – physical, emotional or spiritual – it is important that we try to release the poisonous effects of negative emotions such as bitterness, resentment and guilt, by forgiving those who have hurt us. If we persist with our grudges then ultimately there is the potential that this mind-set will cause us harm. The following short verse illustrates this idea and captures the benefits of releasing our negative emotions.

> For resentment is negative
> Resentment is poisonous
> Resentment diminishes
> And devours the self.
> Be the first to forgive
> To smile and take the first step
> And you will see the happiness bloom
> On the face of your brother or sister.
>
> Be always the first
> Do not wait for others to forgive
> For by forgiving
> You become the master of fate

The fashioner of life
The doer of miracles.

To forgive is the highest
Most beautiful form of love.
In return you will receive
Untold peace and happiness.

From the bookmark Decide to Forgive, by
Dr Robert Muller of the United Nations.

Prayer of St Francis

Lord
Make me an instrument of your peace
Where there is hatred let me sow love
Where there is injury, pardon
Where there is doubt, faith
Where there is despair, hope
Where there is darkness, light
Where there is sadness, joy

O Divine Master
Grant that I may not so much
Seek to be consoled, as to console
To be understood, as to understand
To be loved, as to love
For it is in giving that we receive
It is in pardoning that we are pardoned
It is in dying that we are born to eternal life

7
Trust and Hope

Trust and Hope

Trust and hope are strong components of spirituality. What is spirituality? It is a word that many Christians shy away from because they feel that it is perhaps related to mysticism and even to the occult. This is not at all true. Spirituality, like the word 'faith' considered earlier, has many meanings and I will only suggest one or two here. At the risk of over-simplification, I believe that spirituality is about being in touch with your heart and soul and being attuned to God's 'small voice within'. Spirituality also suggests the ability to find peace and happiness in an imperfect world, and to realize that one's own personality is imperfect but acceptable. Acceptance, faith, forgiveness, peace and love, as well as hope and trust, are traits that define spirituality. There is a very poignant illustration of trust and hope in the most terrible circumstance that took place in World War 2. Allied soldiers found the following message scratched on a basement wall:

I believe in the sun – even when it does not shine
I believe in love – even when it is not shown
I believe in God – even when he does not speak

Time and again in the Bible we find examples of people who knew the meaning of hope and trust. Nowhere is this subject more fully explored than in the beautiful book of Psalms. There, anguish, puzzlement and anger with God stand alongside acceptance, surrender to God's will and, ultimately, thanksgiving. Read the despair of Psalm 22, 'My God, my God, why have you forsaken me?' with Psalm 23, 'The Lord is my shepherd, I shall not be in want.' At the end of all the Psalms there is hope and trust in a living and powerful God.

The following extract challenges us to live in a state of trust, faith and hope that God is in complete control even when we have little understanding of the present, yet alone the future.

We receive enlightenment only in proportion as we give ourselves more and more completely to God by humble submission and love. We do not first see, then act: we act, then see . . . and that is why the man who waits to see clearly before he will believe, never starts the journey.

How can we obey without certainty, when plagued by doubts? I have concluded that faith requires obedience without full knowledge. Like Job, like Abraham, I accept that much lies beyond my finite grasp, and yet I choose to trust God anyhow, humbly accepting my position as a creature whose worth and very life depend on God's mercy.

Thomas Merton, No Man is an Island, *Harcourt Brace & Co, 1955, p.241. Quoted in* Reaching For the Invisible God, *Philip Yancey, Harper Collins Zondervan, Grand Rapids, Michigan, 1995. Used with permission.*

A Prayer for Trust

Lord Jesus, I am afraid of the darkness that exists in my
   life.
There are times when I feel so alone on this journey.
There are times when the light has gone out and I am
At the point of succumbing to despair.
I try to escape in all manner of ways.
Yet deep down I know that escaping
Is not the answer to my needs.
Grant me a childlike faith, a total faith.
Help me to walk by faith and not by sight,
Knowing that there is nothing that can separate me
From your love.
I surrender my needs to your loving care.
I know that all things ultimately work together for good
To those who love you and are called
According to your purposes.
We look only to those things that are seen;
Help me to look to those things that are eternal.
May I abandon myself to your will and find perfect peace
Whatever the storms of life may hold.
In Jesus' name I pray.
Amen.

Trust

Trust in the Lord and do good;
Dwell in the land and enjoy safe pasture.
Delight yourself in the Lord
And he will give you the desires of your heart.
Commit your way to the Lord;
Trust in him and he will do this:
He will make your righteousness
Shine like the dawn,
The justice of your cause like the noonday sun.
Be still before the Lord
And wait patiently for him.

(Psalm 37:3–7)

Hope and Healing

C hristians have a sure foundation for having hope in their lives. We know that whatever the length of our days, whatever the sufferings we pass through, Jesus, the shepherd of our lives, has trod that path. He has overcome the world and by his death and resurrection we have the assurance of 'overcoming the world' and meeting our Lord face to face. Hope is inextricably linked to faith and love. A famous nineteenth-century evangelist, Charles Haddon Spurgeon, composed a beautifully concise summary about the connection between faith, hope and love:

> Faith goes up the stairs that love has made and looks out the window that hope has opened.

The eighteenth-century poet and English essayist Oliver Goldsmith wrote:

> Hope, like the glimmering taper's light,
> adorns and cheers our way;
> and still, as darker grows night,
> emits a brighter ray.

There are hundreds of reassuring passages of Scripture about the reasons for 'having a brighter ray'. Here are a few:

For you have been my hope, O Sovereign Lord, my confidence since my youth. From my birth I have relied on you . . . I will ever praise you. (Psalm 71:5–6)

May the God of hope fill you with all joy and peace as you trust in him, so that you may overflow with hope by the power of the Holy Spirit. (Romans 15:13)

O Israel, put your hope in the Lord, for with the Lord is unfailing love and with him is full redemption. (Psalm 130:7)

Letting Go and Letting God – A Prayer and a Meditation

Dear God,
I want so much to be in control.
I want to be the master of my own destiny.
Still I know that you are saying:
'Let me take you by the hand and lead you.
Accept my love and trust that where I bring you,
the deepest desires of your heart will be fulfilled.'
Lord, open my hands to receive your gift of love.
Through Jesus' name I pray.
Amen.

Excerpted from With Open Hands
by Henri Nouwen © 1995 Ave Maria Press,
Notre Dame, Indiana. Used with permission of the publisher.

Question for Meditation

In what ways am I afraid of dependence on God?

The Healing Within

In wisdom, Providence allowed this illness
To open wide the window of my heart – wide
Enough that Love might come into the stillness.
Like a butterfly, Love landed by my side.
Imperceptibly, as if in a chrysalis state,
I saw its colours beautiful and clear:
Blue, green, yellow and even slate.
Love bade me let go of all my fear.
Love suggested surrendering the past;
To see this as a sacrament of hope and healing.
Happiness, like a tiny lotus flower, came at last.
Wistful first, then quite wonderful, this feeling,
This surging tide, this energy wherein the Kingdom
    dwells.

Paul Kraus

8

Being Positive and Joyful

Happiness and Joy

We tend to use these words interchangeably yet there is an important difference in their meaning. Happiness denotes a transitory feeling, whereas joy and enthusiasm come from the heart, from the soul. People strive to achieve happiness in all kinds of ways. Some seek it in building successful careers, others in the attainment of wealth and all that goes with the acquisition of creature comforts and status symbols. It would appear that happiness is dependent on our fluctuating outward circumstances. In contrast, joy has to do with our 'inner climate', our state of being, our relationship to God.

In the book of Proverbs we read, 'A cheerful heart is good medicine, but a crushed spirit dries up the bones' (Proverbs 17:22). These words confirm the therapeutic value of a joyful spirit. In the New Testament we find further teaching about joy. Jesus said to his disciples, 'I have told you this so that my joy may be in you and that your joy may be complete' (John 15:11).

St Paul talks about joy in a different way: 'Rejoice in the Lord always. I will say it again: Rejoice!' (Philippians 4:4). There are dozens of references to joy and happiness throughout the Bible. God wants us to be joyful and happy. Furthermore, to live joyfully enhances our health, a fact endorsed by medical science.

When we are at peace with ourselves it follows that we can more easily be at peace with God. Helen Keller, that remarkable American lady who was deaf, dumb and blind from childhood, was still able to conquer these fearful disabilities and find joy in her life. She experienced the love of others and was able to give love in return. Furthermore, she set goals in her life – goals centred on communicating with others. Joy and love are of course twins. The Psalmist said, 'Shout for joy to the Lord, all the earth. Worship the Lord with gladness; come before him with joyful songs' (Psalm 100:1–2). Living joyously is no guarantee against suffering but Jesus promised to be with us always, 'even to the very end of the age' (Matthew 28:20).

Joy, then, has much to do with knowing God, walking in his ways and experiencing his peace. Joy comes from within our hearts. It is a spring that never runs dry because it comes from walking with our Lord.

Bringing Healing into Focus – a Matter of Choice

In most areas of life we are confronted with choice. Even when we are faced with illness we can choose to adopt a healing state of mind. Attitude is a vital component of healing. How do we focus our mind for healing? Here are a few suggestions.

- **Focus on acceptance**. We need to be certain that God's love for us is unconditional. His love was so strong that he sent his only Son to make atonement for our sins. The Bible says that 'by his stripes we are healed'. This alone calls us to accept ourselves the way we are in thankful humility and trust.

- **Focus on the positives of life**. Remember that your emotional state is reflected in your physical state.

- **Focus on living lovingly, peacefully and joyously**. In his bestselling book, *Peace, Love & Healing*, Dr Bernie Siegel, MD has said that when you possess these positive emotions every cell in your body responds and you heal more quickly. The famous seventeenth-century English poet George Herbert wrote, 'Thou hast given me so much/ Give one thing more, a grateful heart.' Indeed, a grateful, loving heart is a heart open to healing.

- **Focus on forgiving.** You cannot live peacefully or joyfully if you are burdened with anger, guilt and for ever judging people. Pray that God might remove any such destructive feelings. Try (and if necessary seek help) to release the hidden hurts that might be plaguing your life.

- **Focus on others.** Self-centredness is also a block to healing. Thinking about others helps us to forget our own problems and gives us a different outlook on life.

Inner Attitude – A Barometer of Our Health

A cheerful heart is good medicine, but a crushed spirit dries up the bones. (Proverbs 17:22)

These words from the Bible have a timeless ring of truth about them. Healing is facilitated when we are spiritually well, when there is balance in our life and an absence of inner strife. We sometimes tend to forget that we have a choice when we face adversity.

Our emotional health is closely determined by our inner attitudes and state of mind. It is a well known fact that the majority of patients seen by general practitioners have stress-related illnesses that in a large measure are due (either directly or indirectly) to negative attitudes. A famous American cardiologist, Dr Dean Ornish, has conducted many well publicized studies that have demonstrated how the attitudes we hold do not stay as mere attitudes but eventually have physical effects in one form or another, most commonly in illness.

God has so made us that the right attitudes produce the right effects in our bodies. Many passages of Scripture confirm this truth. One of the bluntest biblical passages is found in Jeremiah, who wrote: 'The heart is deceitful above all things, and desperately corrupt; who can understand it? I the Lord search the mind and try the heart, to give every man according to his ways, according to the fruit of his doings' (Jeremiah 17:9–10 RSV).

Jesus reflected a similar sentiment when he said: 'But what comes out of the mouth proceeds from the heart, and this defiles a man. For out of the heart come evil thoughts, murder, adultery, fornication, theft, false witness, slander. These are what defile a man, but to eat with unwashed hands does not defile a man' (Matthew 15:19–20 RSV).

These passages, and many others, point directly to the fact that health and illness have a connection with the state of our heart – to our inner state and to the attitudes we hold. That is not, of course, for one moment to suggest that there is always a causal link between illness and the state of our emotions. Many illnesses have their origins in environmental, genetic or other factors. Nevertheless, when we are at peace with ourselves and the world, that peace helps to maintain our overall balance and good health. When Jesus healed the man who was paralysed, he also released that man from a burdened conscience: 'Take heart . . . your sins are forgiven' (Matthew 9:2). With these words Jesus indicated that physical and emotional healing go hand in hand.

It is an interesting fact that one of the best-selling books of the twentieth century was *The Power of Positive Thinking* by Dr Norman Vincent Peale. Remember that God has so designed us that the right attitudes produce the right effects in our bodies.

9

Practising the Presence of God

The Antidote to Stress

We live in a noisy world. Little wonder then that we feel ill-at-ease when confronted by silence. Our lives are so often overcrowded – sometimes by our own choosing, at other times due to circumstances beyond our control. We seek inner peace and quiet but frequently fail to find it.

Depression is rife and the taking of antidepressants is probably the most common form of medication in the Western world today. Living more mindfully, being more in touch with ourselves and paying attention to what our heart is telling us, would help us in our quest for peace of mind. If we take time to pause amid the hectic pace of life we will begin to realize that life is immersed in mystery and is often much more than it seems. Jesus' promise remains as true as ever, 'My peace I give to you; not as the world gives do I give to you' (John 14:27 RSV).

Meditation and contemplative prayer (both of which foster mindfulness) seem to have become quite foreign to our experience. Many people are prejudiced towards such a 'non-doing' potentially mindless activity. This is a pity because if this is the case we have lost sight of a valuable part of our Christian heritage. Meditation and contemplative prayer have historically been important expressions of our Christian spirituality. In this neglect we have lost the simple wisdom and spiritual perception by which we can better know ourselves and therefore the Christ who dwells in us, through the Holy Spirit.

Jesus himself emphasized the need for this inward orientation on various occasions throughout his life and ministry. In Mark's Gospel (6:31 RSV) he said to his disciples, 'Come away by yourselves to a lonely place, and rest a while.' It seems as though at times we are almost incapable of letting go our incessant 'doing' and allowing ourselves just 'to be'; to just rest in God's presence – a God who knows our needs before we ask, and our frailty in asking.

The paradox of Christian meditation is that although it is a turning inwards, our focus is not on ourselves and our preoccupations, but on the ultimate transforming power of God. When we are in silence before God we will learn to experience the indwelling Spirit. In learning to be still before God we become more focused, more sensitive to the sacred. Being still before God is simplicity itself yet its effects on our life can be profound. We begin to listen to what our heart is telling us. The experience of coming before the Lord in stillness will eventually flow into every aspect of our life.

A Suggested Meditation

Read a Bible verse that speaks of peace and healing. Examples include:

Psalm 23: 'The Lord is my Shepherd.'
Psalm 46:10: 'Be still, and know that I am God.'
Psalm 103:1 'Bless the Lord, O my soul.'

With your eyes closed, slowly repeat your chosen verse and let its meaning sink in. Spend a few minutes repeating this verse, allowing its meaning to reach down into your subconscious. Then focus your awareness on the feeling of peace that this verse has brought you.

REMEMBER: Christian meditation is, in essence, contemplative prayer; it is a devotional exercise. In the fifteenth century, St Thomas à Kempis wrote in *The Imitation of Christ*:

Turn then to God . . . devote yourself to those things that are within, and you will see the Kingdom of God come unto you, that Kingdom which is peace and joy in the Holy Spirit.

Meditation and Silent Prayer – Shhh . . . God's Talking

Practising the presence of God in silence can take many forms. One is to sit quietly and say a simple prayer in one's mind. Silent prayer can be particularly beneficial when we are troubled, confused or need inspiration, or simply when we need to experience the peace of God. Contrary to what some Christians believe, meditation is not emptying the mind but learning to still the mind. It is not 'navel gazing' but rather focused awareness, usually on a Scriptural phrase. Meditation, as the following practice suggests, is all about becoming more aware of the presence of God in our life. It is a highly therapeutic spiritual exercise and has shown to be so down through the centuries of Christian history.

Entering the Silence

First, it must be said that there are no rules as to how long you need to spend in meditation or contemplative prayer. The important thing is the quality of the time spent in quietness. Cardinal John Henry Newman once said that in the quiet 'there is a stillness that speaks'. He also noted the strangeness of perfect silence after continued sound. How do we enter this 'sacred silence'? Here are a few guidelines:

(1) Phase of relaxation

Just sit down, maintaining a comfortable, but not too comfortable, posture, making sure that you relax the body, but at the same time keeping inwardly alert. Now, take a few deep, 'letting go' breaths. Breathe out tension, anxiety and worry. With your eyes closed, visualize any tension melting away. Let your mind, heart, will and feelings become tranquil and serene. It may well be that you spend your entire time in this phase. If this is the case then don't let it worry you. It is in times of peace and silence that we allow the grace of God to pour into our hearts and it is at such times that we surrender to his will.

(2) Phase of awareness of God's presence

In the stillness be assured that God knows you better than you know yourself. God is the one in whom we live and move and have our being. Through Jesus we are able to call God 'Abba', Father. In this phase our hearts come to God in full confidence that he is with us now. We surrender our wills to God's will so that Christ can reign in our hearts. We accept Jesus as Sovereign Lord and put ourselves in his control. We put aside self and enthrone Jesus in our hearts.

(3) Phase of forgiveness

If we have a sense of guilt, shame or fear, if we have a sense of unworthiness before God, our heavenly Father, we need to remove that barrier. One writer has said that it is a healing grace to surrender our sinfulness to his mercy.

(4) Phase of contemplation

With pure hearts, in response to God's love, we can 'rest in the presence of the Lord'. We can do this by means of a scriptural phrase, already suggested, or by listening to our breath as a means of moving into stillness; or by repeating a 'sacred' word. At the end of this period of contemplative prayer, sit in silence for a few minutes, allowing yourself to slowly emerge from this peaceful experience.

A Prayer for Silence

Dear Lord,
Grant me the serenity and the will
To keep times of silence each day.
May the noises of daily life be hushed
So that you can speak to me
In the silence of my heart.
Even when my chattering mind
Drowns the quietness, Lord,
Grant me the faith to persevere
And to know that I can never leave your presence.
May I hear your still, small voice
Calling 'Come unto me all who are heavy laden
And I will give you rest, for I am gentle
And lowly in heart . . .'
Let your voice of Love for ever be my guide.
O Lamb of God, I come.
Amen

Christ Within Us – the Hope of Glory

There are many verses in Scripture that tell us we are made in the likeness of God's image and that he dwells within each one of us. What follows is a small selection of Bible verses that remind us that our lives are incomplete when we forget or ignore the power of the transcendent God who dwells within.

> Do you not know that your body is a temple of the Holy Spirit, who is in you, whom you have received from God? (1 Corinthians 6:19)

> Let the peace of Christ rule in your hearts, since as members of one body you were called to peace. And be thankful. Let the word of Christ dwell in you richly as you teach and admonish one another in all wisdom, and as you sing psalms, hymns and spiritual songs with gratitude in your hearts to God. (Colossians 3:15–16)

> No-one has ever seen God; but if we love one another, God lives in us and his love is made complete in us. . . God is love. Whoever lives in love lives in God, and God in him. (1 John 4:12, 16)

10

Ultimate Healing — To Be With the Lord

The Mystery of Healing

Jesus heals today. This is the reality of Christian experience and we regularly read and hear of wondrous ways the Lord heals today. At the same time we hear of much suffering in our midst. Sometimes people are healed; sometimes this is not the case, despite a great outpouring of prayer. This, then, is the paradox of the Christian experience. Yet, in the midst of this apparent contradiction we need to remind ourselves that Jesus does indeed care about us and heal us of our hurts. Again and again the Bible reminds us of this comforting fact. We are told: 'cast all your anxiety on him because he cares for you' (1 Peter 5:7). Jesus promised us, 'I am with you always, even to the very end of the age' (Matthew 28:20).

The most we can say about the mind of Christ in regard to healing is that he always wants the best for us. Healing was at the core of Jesus' earthly ministry, whether it was manifest in a physical cure or in the restoration of a person's relationship with God in the forgiveness of sin. In praying for healing we need to remember that prayer is asking God for the power to do his will, not our will. This can be a difficult thing to do when we are fervently seeking a healing for someone who is close to us. We need to pray for a fuller knowledge and discernment in a particular situation.

If we are to be used by God to bring healing to others, we need to listen carefully to what God may be saying to us in the beauty and sanctity of silence. We should also expect to receive an answer to prayer, whatever that answer may be. We may not always see the higher purpose God has in a particular situation. We cannot allow our own preoccupations and agenda to get in the way of God's purposes.

> 'My grace is sufficient for you, for my power is made perfect in weakness' . . . For when I am weak, then I am strong. (2 Corinthians 12:9–10)

> Therefore we do not lose heart. Though outwardly we are wasting away, yet inwardly we are being renewed day by day. For our light and momentary troubles are achieving for us an eternal glory that far outweighs them all. So we fix our eyes not on what is seen, but on what is unseen. For what is seen is temporary, but what is unseen is eternal. (2 Corinthians 4:16–18)

The person who can interpret their life's circumstances in the terms which Paul describes in these verses from Corinthians is a person who has entered deeply into the mystery of Christ's passion and who knows about the God who can make us whole, not just by a cure but by a cross, not just by taking us out of trouble, but more profoundly by using our trouble and ultimately our death as the appointed path to wholeness of life with him.

Each of the above verses gives us deep assurance that

though our mortal nature is so fragile and subject to all kinds of suffering, yet beneath us are the everlasting arms that will never let us go, until ultimately we will meet the Lord and reign with him in glory.

For to me, to live is Christ and to die is gain. (Philippians 1:21)

My flesh and my heart may fail, but God is the strength of my heart and my portion for ever. (Psalm 73:26)

Ultimate Healing – to be with the Lord

Death is a sad parting, but in the course of time it will seem that I have only slipped away into the next room. Whatever we were to each other, that we are still. Call me by my old familiar name, speak of me in the easy way you always used. Laugh as we always laughed at the little jokes we enjoyed together. Play, smile, think of me, pray for me. Let my name be the household word that it always was. Let it be spoken of without effort. Life means all that it ever meant. It is the same as it ever was; there is an absolute unbroken continuity. Why should I be out of your mind because I am out of your sight?

I am but waiting for you, for an interval, somewhere very near, just around the corner. All is well. Nothing of value has been lost; in the fullness of time all will be as it was before – only infinitely more peaceful and forever – for we will be one together with Christ.

Canon Henry Scott Holland, 1847–1918.
Onetime Dean of St Paul's Cathedral, London.

A Prayer for Those Who Have Gone Before Us

Holy and loving Father, you gave us life when you created us, and in your redeeming love you have given us new life in Christ Jesus. We give you thanks for [name]. In faith and trust we leave [her/him] in your keeping, through Jesus Christ our Lord, who died and rose again to save us, and now lives and reigns with you and the Holy Spirit in glory for ever. Amen

Our Victory Over Death – Words of Great Consolation

We know that in everything God works for good with those who love him, who are called according to his purpose. . . .Who shall separate us from the love of Christ? Shall tribulation, or distress, or persecution, or famine, or nakedness, or peril, or sword? . . . No, in all these things we are more than conquerors through him who loved us. For I am sure that neither death, nor life, nor angels, nor principalities, nor things present, nor things to come, nor powers, nor height, nor depth, nor anything else in all creation, will be able to separate us from the love of God in Christ Jesus our Lord. (Romans 8:28, 35, 37 RSV)

A Holy Moment

The following poem represents a Christian perspective on the moment of death – a moment when we are born to eternal life. This is a gift, the Christian believes, which Christ gained through his death and resurrection, thus once and for all destroying our need to fear death. St Paul expressed this fact succinctly when he wrote 'that the perishable will put on the imperishable. And the mortal puts on immortality'.

> When striving ceases, when ego dies,
> When only praise and alleluias rise,
> When I awake on Resurrection's morn,
> When I shall glimpse that glorious dawn.
>
> Then shall I see my Master's face
> And stand in His amazing grace.
> Unceasing love forever free –
> It is this Lord who died for me.
>
> A holy moment that will be,
> Sheer ecstasy to be set free
> From tyranny of self; from fear
> And doubt; anxiety ever near.

A holy moment that will be
To meet the angels and to see
Loved ones from this veil of tears,
There to dwell beyond all years.

No more hunger, no more thirst,
Then the last shall be the first,
Then this puzzling tapestry –
Profound in its eternity.

A holy moment that will be!

Paul Kraus